WHY SHOULD I HELP?

HODDER
Wayland

WHY SHOULD I?

WHY SHOULD I Eat Well?
WHY SHOULD I Help?
WHY SHOULD I Listen?
WHY SHOULD I Share?

Published in Great Britain in 2001 by Hodder Wayland,
an imprint of Hodder Children's Books
© Copyright 2001 Hodder Wayland

Commissioning editor: Alex Woolf
Editor: Liz Gogerly
Designer: Jean Wheeler
Digital Colour: Carl Gordon

British Library Cataloguing in Publication Data
Llewellyn, Claire
Why should I help?
1. Helping behaviour – Juvenile literature
I.Title II.Help
158.3

ISBN 0 7502 3642 6

Printed and bound in Italy by G. Canale & C.Sp.A., Turin

Hodder Children's Books
A division of Hodder Headline Limited
338 Euston Road, London NW1 3BH

WHY SHOULD I HELP?

Written by Claire Llewellyn

Illustrated by Mike Gordon

HODDER
Wayland

an imprint of Hodder Children's Books

Every morning, at my house,
there are jobs to be done.

Making the beds ...

4

feeding the pets ...

and clearing away
the breakfast.

5

And there are more jobs to do in the evening. Laying the table ...

washing up ...

and helping to run
the bath for Charlie.

Sometimes I don't feel like helping.
I want to do something else instead.
Finish a drawing ...

watch TV ...

Why should I help other people?
No one ever helps me!

Dad said, 'Everyone needs a helping hand now and then. Remember what happened when you fell off your bike?'

'That nice boy helped you back home.'

'Mum cycled home in her lunch hour to get it.'

'And do you remember what happened that day you lost Squeaky?'

Ahhh, Squeaky's gone!

'Ben, Grandad, Gran
and I searched for him
the whole afternoon.'

18

It was all true.
I did sometimes need
a helping hand.
And I suppose other people
need one, too.

When they're busy ...

or tired …

or just a bit slow.

I'll get it!

People help one another all the time.

So I'm going to help people too.
Helping people makes me feel grown-up,
and gives me a good feeling inside.

23

And sometimes, just sometimes,
there's an extra bonus.
Because I went to the shops for
my Gran ...

she had time to make
some pancakes.

And because I fed the fish
for Ben ...

he brought me back a present from his holiday.

All sorts of people need
help out there.
So give someone
a helping hand.

Who knows?
The next person
to need help
might be you!

Notes for parents and teachers

Why Should I? and the National Curriculum

The Why Should I? series satisfies a number of requirements for the *Personal, Social and Health Education non-statutory framework at Key Stage 1.* Within the category *Developing confidence and responsibility,* these books will help young readers to recognize what they like and dislike, what is fair and unfair, and what is right and wrong; to think about themselves, learn from their experiences and recognize what they are good at. Under *Developing a healthy, safer lifestyle,* some of the titles in this series will help to teach children how to make simple choices that improve their health and well-being, to maintain personal hygiene, and to learn rules for, and ways of, keeping safe, including basic road safety. Under *Developing good relationships and respecting the differences between people,* reading these books will help children to recognize how their behaviour affects other people, to listen to other people and play and work cooperatively, and that family and friends should care for each other.

Why Should I Help?

Why Should I Help? is intended to be an enjoyable book that discusses the importance of helping other people. A variety of situations throughout this book explore the value of helping children move in different worlds – in the family, their school and their neighbourhood. Helping other people encourages children to become active members of their communities. Communities are built by people helping one another and making a contribution. Taking an active part in family life prepares children for becoming active members of society.

Helping other people is a way of forming and strengthening relationships. It is important that children see and understand how family members care for one another. Giving a hand to lay the table, play with the baby or feed the rabbit are a recognition of the give-and-take nature of family life.

Helping at home or at school is one of the ways in which children begin to take responsibility for themselves. Hanging up their clothes or clearing up the classroom are signs that children are moving from dependency towards independence and responsibility.

Recognizing when people need help is an important step in learning about other people's feelings. Children need to become aware of the needs of other people, whatever their age. Of course, it is vital that children are thanked for their help. Positive feedback makes children feel good about themselves and enhances their self-esteem.

Suggestions as you read the book with children

As you read this book with children, stop now and again to discuss the issues raised in the text. Do they have to do jobs around the house? How do they feel about this? Think about all the jobs their mum or dad do. Do their parents enjoy doing these jobs? Are there some jobs they really hate?

Look at the examples given in the text when Susy needed help. Has something similar ever happened to them? Was somebody there to help them?

There is a police officer in this book. Police officers are just some of the people in uniform who are there to help us. Can they think of any others? Why is a uniform so useful? Can they imagine a time when they might need to seek help for themselves?

Suggested follow-up activities

Plan a group task, such as making a model, which might entail helping other pupils or friends.

Ask them to draw up a list of things they can do by themselves and things for which they need help. Why are there some things they can do alone and other things they can't?

What words or phrases or sayings can they think of to do with helping. What do people mean when they say the following?

Many hands make light work   Help yourself
Too many cooks spoil the broth   Helpline
Lend a hand   Helpmate
Every little helps   First aid

Books to read

Katie Morag Delivers the Mail by Moira Hedderwick (Red Fox, 1997)
A picture book about a little girl on a Scottish island
who delivers the mail because the postmistress,
her mother, is too busy with a new baby.

It's your turn Roger by Susanna Gretz
(Red Fox, 1996)
A picture book about Roger the pig who
doesn't like to help around the house.

When Mum Turned into a Monster
by Joanna Harrison (Collins Picture Lions)
A picture book about two naughty children
who do not help their mother.